THE DRUMMER'S SOURCEBOOK

OVER 60 POPULAR RHYTHMS
IN STANDARD NOTATION

Wise Publications
part of The Music Sales Group
London / New York / Paris / Sydney / Copenhagen / Berlin / Madrid / Hong Kong / Tokyo

Published by
Wise Publications
14-15 Berners Street, London W1T 3LJ, UK.

Exclusive Distributors:
Music Sales Limited
Distribution Centre, Newmarket Road, Bury St Edmunds, Suffolk IP33 3YB, UK.
Music Sales Pty Limited
20 Resolution Drive, Caringbah, NSW 2229, Australia.

Order No. AM1003013
ISBN: 978-1-84938-991-4
This book © Copyright 2011 Wise Publications, a division of Music Sales Limited.

Edited by Adrian Hopkins
Cover and Book Design by Fresh Lemon

Printed in the EU

CD recorded and mixed by Jonas Persson
Drums and additional music editing by Noam Lederman

Your Guarantee of Quality
As publishers, we strive to produce every book to the highest commercial standards.
This book has been carefully designed to minimise awkward
page turns and to make playing from it a real pleasure.
Particular care has been given to specifying acid-free, neutral-sized paper
made from pulps which have not been elemental chlorine bleached.
This pulp is from farmed sustainable forests and was produced with special regard for the environment.
Throughout, the printing and binding have been planned to ensure a sturdy,
attractive publication which should give years of enjoyment.
If your copy fails to meet our high standards, please inform us and we will gladly replace it.

www.musicsales.com

CONTENTS

INTRODUCTION

Welcome to *Rhythm Guides: The Drummers Sourcebook.* This book is meant not as a method, but rather as a reference guide for all percussion players and enthusiasts, and provides insight into the most popular rhythms from around the globe, presented for both beginners and advanced players alike. Knowledge of these rhythms will add to your versatility and broaden your expertise in different styles.

While it is difficult to outline the authenticity of all rhythms (due to the many variations of each), this guide contains the most common and practical ways to play each one.

How to Use This Book

It is strongly recommended that you develop a practice regimen in which you devote some time to learning each rhythm. Play each pattern several times until you can master the "groove" of each one. Listen to the CD to fully appreciate the intricacies of many of the rhythms. Use a metronome, and practice at several tempos until you can play each rhythm at different speeds.

Format

The rhythms and patterns are presented in alphabetical order. Every rhythm is written in standard drumset, and to emphasise the rhythmic subtleties, the samba percussion chart is included as well. Most of the rhythms are notated as repeated two-bar patterns. This book also includes a tuning and maintenance section packed with tips to help keep your equipment in good condition. Enjoy!

KIT KEY

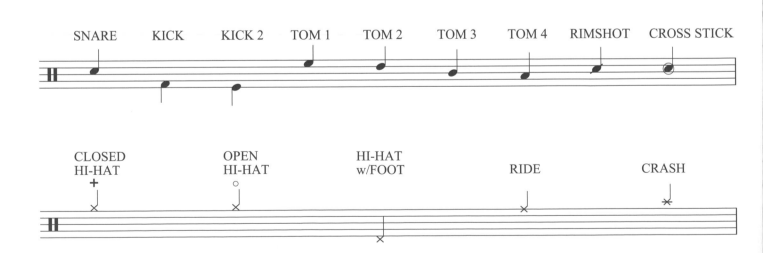

AFRICAN (ABAKWA)

Abakwa is the most popular African rhythm. It is usually played on different drums, especially on the side of the drums, in order to get a wood-like sound.

BLUES

Blues is one of the most celebrated forms of American music and comes from the mixture of Negro spirituals, dance music and chants. It started as a type of a cappella folk song, and has since evolved into different forms of instrumentation. The standard blues form is known as a "12-bar blues," and the triplet-based *shuffle* can be notated in simple meter with triplets ($\frac{4}{4}$) or in compound meter ($\frac{12}{8}$).

Basic 12-bar blues progression

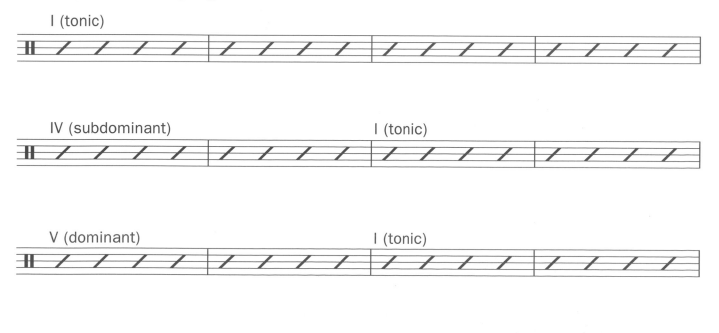

BLUES (continued)

2 CD TRACK · CD TRACK · CD TRACK

Standard Shuffle

Shuffle in $\frac{4}{4}$

$\quad \boldsymbol{\downarrow} = 124$

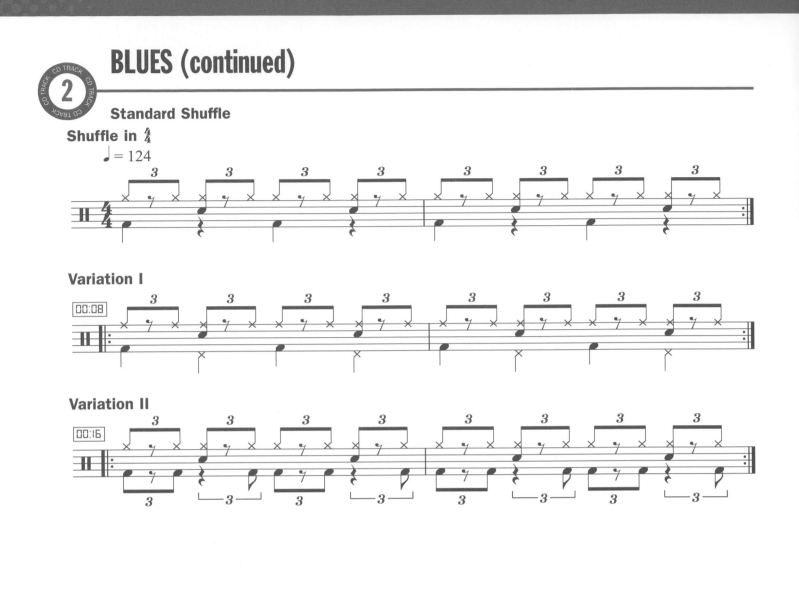

Variation I

`00:08`

Variation II

`00:16`

3

Slow Blues in 12/8

♩. = 80

Variation

00:18

4

Chicago Shuffle in 4/4

♩ = 105

loose hats

Variation

00:10

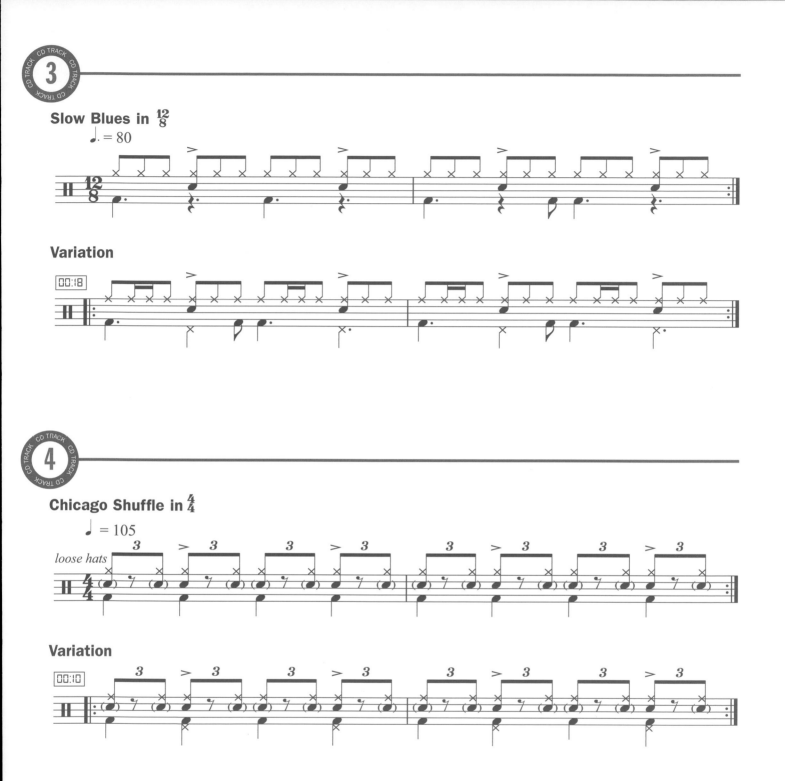

BLUES (continued)

CD TRACK 5

Upbeat Shuffle in $\frac{4}{4}$

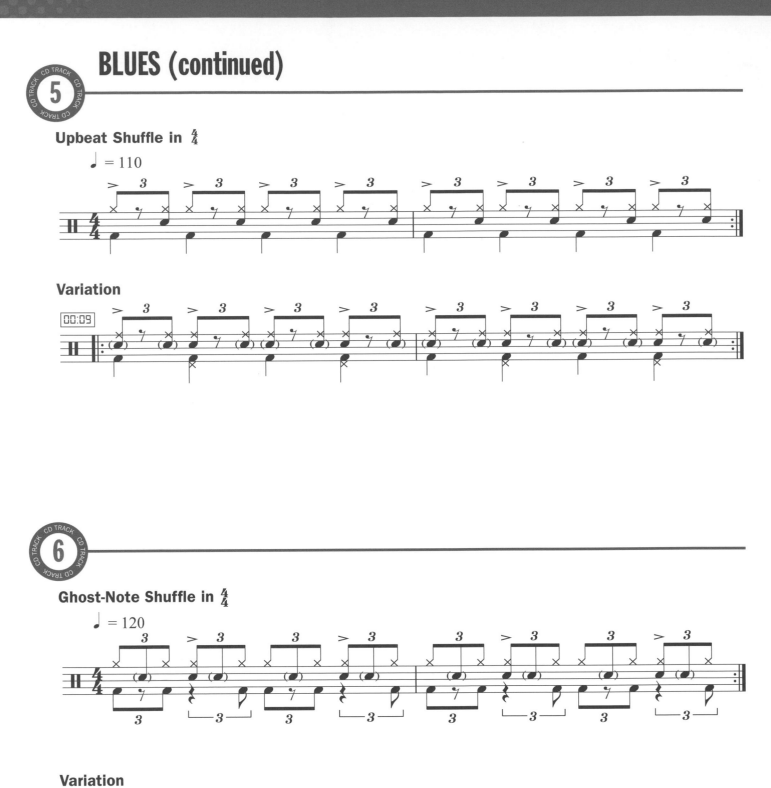

Variation

Ghost-Note Shuffle in $\frac{4}{4}$

CD TRACK 6

Variation

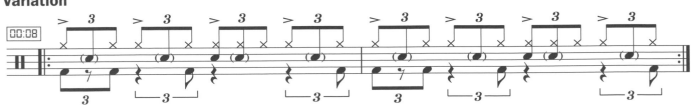

BOLERO

CD TRACK 7

This rhythm was started in Cuba at the end of the nineteenth century. It is a kind of slow *son,* generally played in a ballad-style tempo. This rhythm is based on the Cuban clave rhythm. One of its more important ambassadors was Beny Moré.

Bolero in 4/4

♩ = 100

CD TRACK 8

Bolero in 3/4

♩ = 74

BOSSA NOVA

CD TRACK 9

This rhythm is a combination of *samba de salão* (a 2/4 rhythm with accents on beat 1) and *canção* ("song"), which is a Portuguese-based style. The mixture of these two, along with the influences of jazz and of Cuban bolero, gave rise to the *bossa nova,* which is usually played by small ensembles that consist mainly of a singer accompanied by guitar, piano and drums.

Basic Rhythm in 4/4

♩ = 135

Variation

00:07

CAJUN

Cajun is a folk rhythm that emerged from the French-Canadian influence during the 18th century in New Orleans, Louisiana. These rhythms are usually played on a drumset.

Cajun

Variation

Waltz in 3

Variation

Slow in 9

Variation

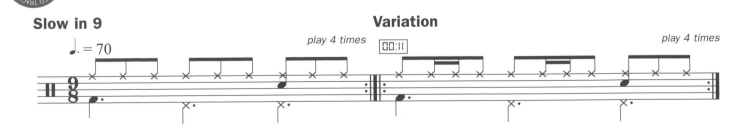

CALYPSO

Calypso is a French rhythm that originated in the Caribbean islands (most notably Trinidad) during the 1950s. Calypso was a folk-type song form originally played by large ensembles until the appearance of steel drums. Nowadays, the calypso rhythm can be heard both in steel drum ensembles and in other different small-group bands.

Calypso

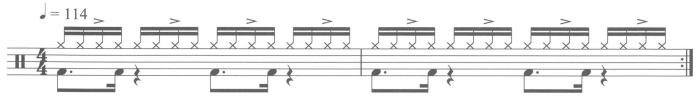

Variation I

Variation II

COUNTRY

This style of folk music originated in the United States through the influence of Irish and Scottish immigrants, and originally revolved around instruments like the fiddle and the banjo. Here are some of the most representative examples of country music:

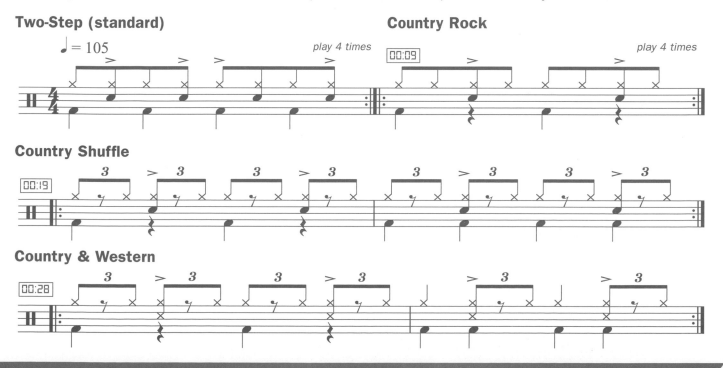

COUNTRY (continued)

15

Country Ballad

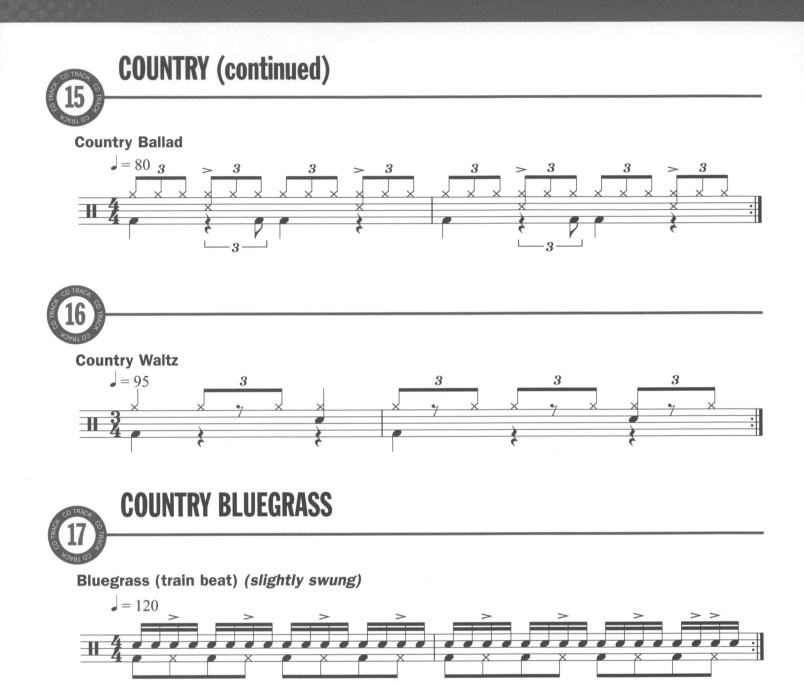

16

Country Waltz

COUNTRY BLUEGRASS

17

Bluegrass (train beat) *(slightly swung)*

DISCO

Disco is a rhythm that developed in the mid-seventies. It has its roots in soul and funk music, with elements of rock.

Standard

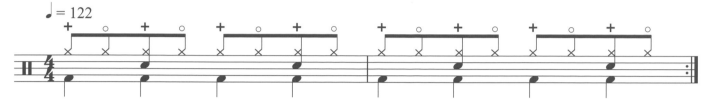

Variation

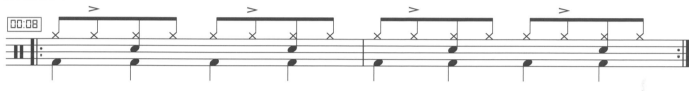

Sixteenths

Variation

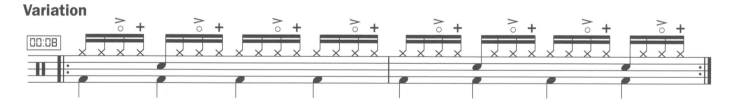

DRUM & BASS

CD TRACK 20

Standard

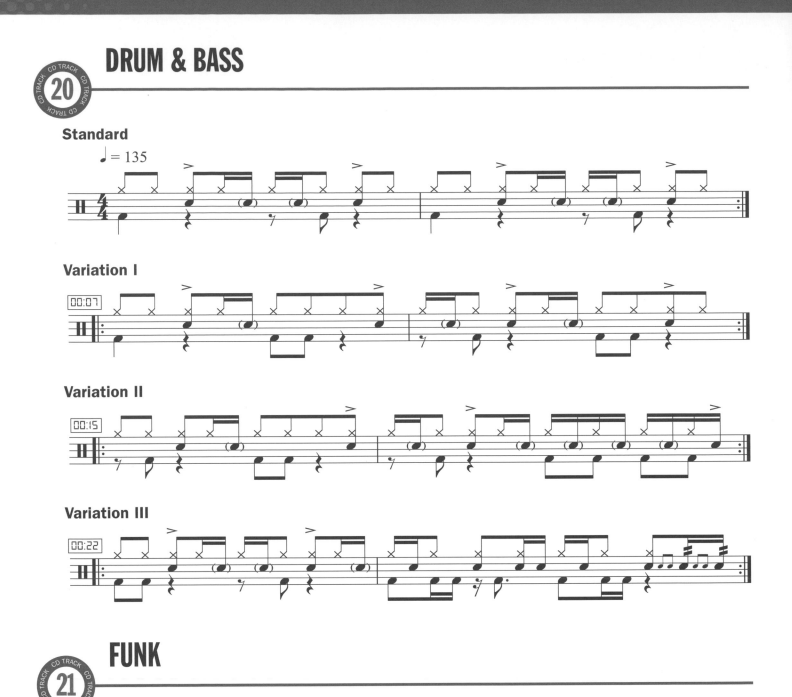

Variation I

Variation II

Variation III

FUNK

CD TRACK 21

Funk is a style that has its roots in jazz, rock and soul music. It is a syncopated rhythm that became popular in the sixties and achieved its peak popularity in the mid-seventies.

Displaced Funk (James Brown Style)

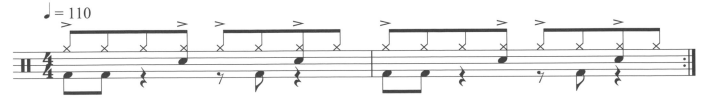

Variation I

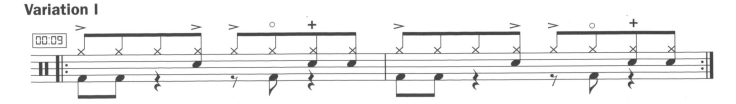

FUNK (continued)

21

Variation II

Variation III

NEW ORLEANS FUNK

22

New Orleans Funk

♩ = 185

Variation I

23

Variation II (Professor Long Hair style)

♩ = 120

FUNK ROCK

24

Standard

Variation I

Variation II

Variation III

LINEAR FUNK

25

Standard Groove

26

Groove I

27

Groove II

28

Groove III

29

GOSPEL

Gospel is an African-American rhythm that has its roots in the blues, and is widely played in African-American Baptist churches. The success of this genre is due in part to the early and consistent promotion of one of its most prominent enthusiasts, Thomas A. Dorsey.

Standard

♩ = 100

Half-Time

00:10

Variation I

00:20

Variation II

00:29

HEAVY METAL

Heavy metal is a fast-tempo music that has its origin in rock. Among its most characteristic features are distorted guitars, challenging rhythms, high-pitched or growling vocals, and double bass drum patterns.

Standard

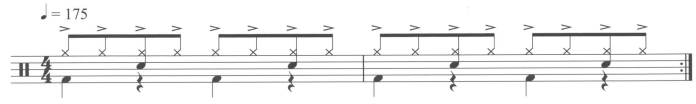

Blast Beat

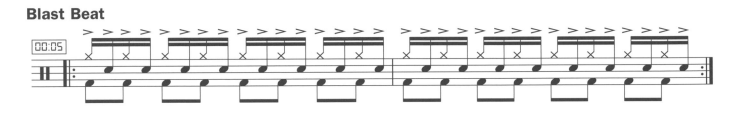

Double Pedal I

Double Pedal II

HEAVY METAL 2

32

'Stoner' Rock

'Sludge' Rock

33

Nu Metal

Rap Metal

HIP-HOP

Hip-hop is a concoction of styles ranging from rhythm & blues to rock and funk. With the increasing popularity of rap in the mid-eighties and the technological revolution of sequencers and drum machines, this style took on a major role on the mainstream music scene. Today, live musicians are becoming a standard element in this music, sometimes even with two drummers playing simultaneously.

Standard

Variation I

Variation II

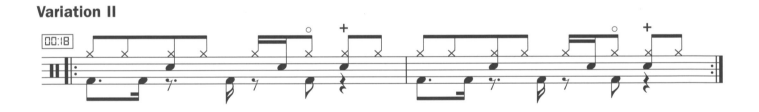

Variation III

HIP-HOP 2

Slow feel

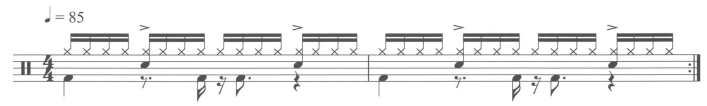

$\quad = 85$

Variation I

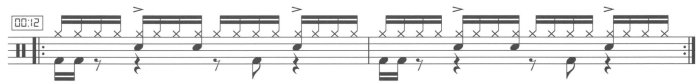

00:12

Variation II

00:23

JAZZ 1

Jazz is the quintessential American music. With its roots in African-American music, jazz is the result of a multifaceted mix of different influences assimilated in New Orleans in the early 1900s, and is characterized by extensive use of the "swing" feel. Some of the main styles of jazz are Dixieland (1900–1920), big band (1920–1950), bebop (1940–1950), cool jazz (1950–1960), and avant-garde (1960s).

Standard Swing Groove

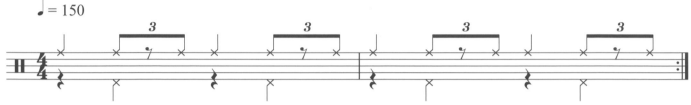

Dixieland

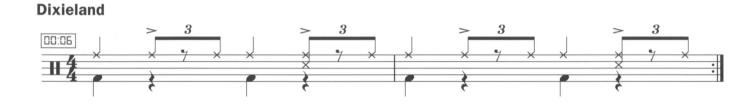

Charleston

Swing

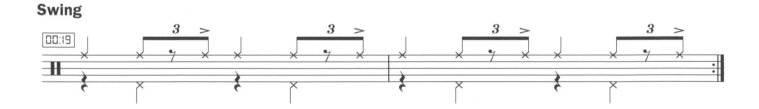

Swing Variation I

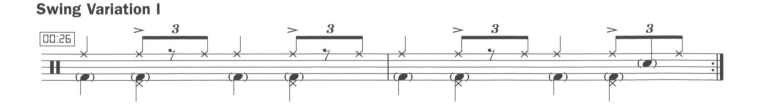

JAZZ 2

CD TRACK 37

Jazz Waltz

Waltz Variation I

Waltz Variation II

KLEZMER

This style comes from the rich musical tradition of the Jewish population of Eastern Europe. The rhythms presented here are adaptations of the traditional rhythms for the drumset. Among the most popular rhythms of this style are the *bulgar*, the *freylakhs*, the *hora*, the *khosidl*, and the *terkisher.*

Bulgar

Variation

Freylakhs

Terkisher

40

Hora

41

Khosidl

MARCH

42

March is the traditional rhythm written for marching in two-step time.
Originally, the march was used for military processions.

March

Variation I

Variation II

MERENGUE

Merengue is a folk dance and rhythm from the Dominican Republic, with strong African and French roots. Merengue has three main parts: merengue, jaleo, and apanpichao. Its typical instrumentation includes tambora, güiro, and accordion.

Merengue

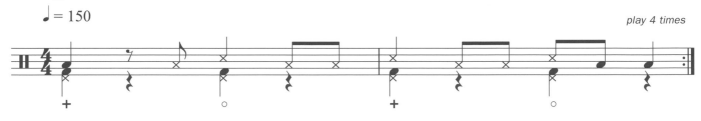

NEW ORLEANS (SECOND LINE)

The *Second Line* used to be (and to some degree still is) a brass and percussion marching band used in parades and/or funerals, depending on the occasion. This rhythm has been adapted to the drumset and is one of the cornerstones of swing.

PROG ROCK

CD TRACK 45

Progressive rock is a subgenre of rock music that sprung from the more imaginative groups of the 60s. It incorporated elements drawn from classical, jazz and world music, and utilised non-standard time signatures, extended improvisatory sections and an emphasis on musicianship.

The term was initially applied to the music of bands such as Pink Floyd, Yes, Genesis and Emerson, Lake & Palmer, reaching its peak of popularity in the mid 1970s.

Prog in 6/4

Variation

CD TRACK 46

Prog in 7/4

Variation

REGGAE (ONE-DROP)

CD TRACK **47**

Reggae is a Jamaican style that has elements of ska, rhythm & blues, and Afro-Jamaican rhythms. It started in the fifties following the popularity of calypso and ska, and became very popular during the sixties and seventies thanks to Bob Marley and the Wailers. The most characteristic feature of this rhythm is the synchronized hit of the bass and snare drum cross-stick (rim) on the third beat.

Standard (shuffle feel)

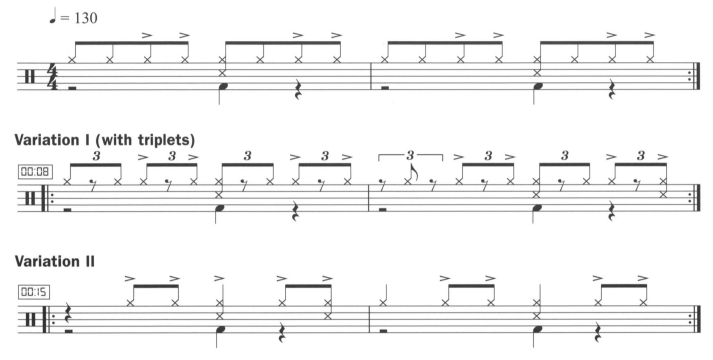

Variation I (with triplets)

Variation II

Variation III

Variation IV

ROCK 1

48

The *rock* beat is the most popular and influential rhythm in pop music. Rock has been around since the fifties, and is a combination of jazz and rhythm & blues. The following examples are just some of the most common and popular rock rhythms.

49

ROCK 2

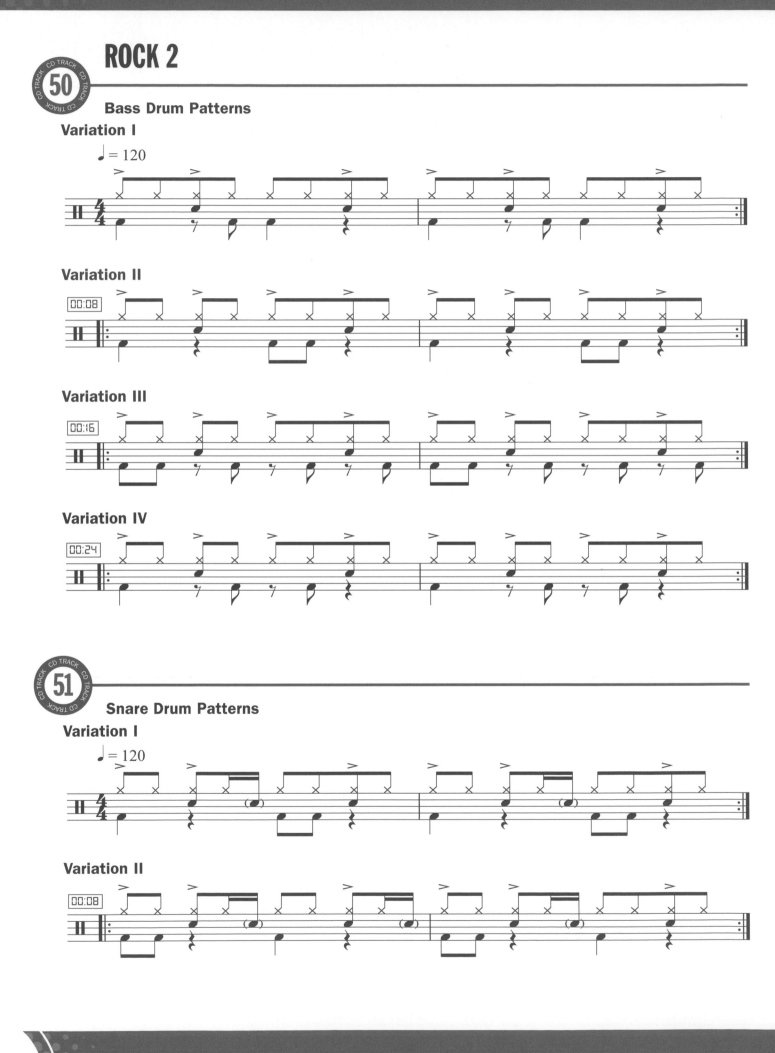

Bass Drum Patterns

Variation I

Variation II

Variation III

Variation IV

Snare Drum Patterns

Variation I

Variation II

51

Variation III

`00:16`

Variation IV

`00:24`

ROCK 3

52

Alternative Rock Patterns

Variation I

♩ = 130

Variation II

`00:07`

Variation III

`00:15`

Variation IV

`00:22`

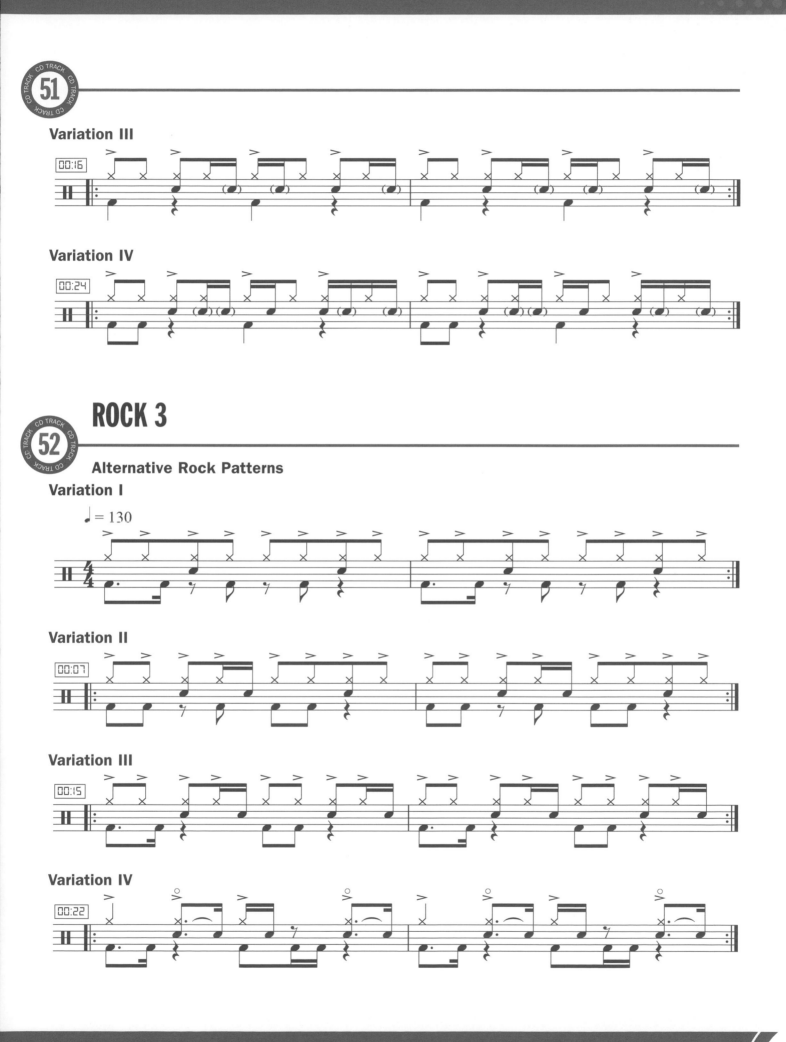

SAMBA

Samba is the most popular Afro-Brazilian rhythm. There are different variations depending on the region, but all of them have their origins in Congolese and Angolan rhythms. The main characteristics of this style include a percussion ensemble consisting of drums, tambourine and cowbells; an accent on the second beat; and $\frac{2}{4}$ meter.

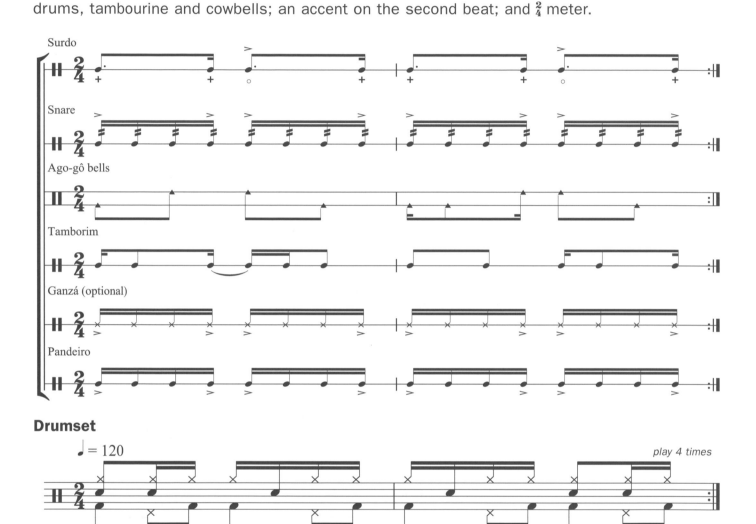

Drumset

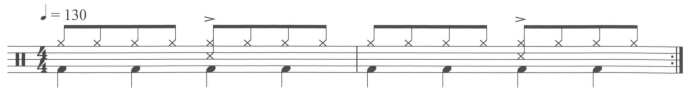

SKA

Ska is a Jamaican rhythm that started in the 1950s, and is a mixture of rock 'n' roll, jazz, and rhythm & blues. Ska's feel is very similar to reggae since both rhythms emphasize the third beat of each measure. Another characteristic of ska is the "four on the floor" pulse in the bass drum.

Standard

Variation I

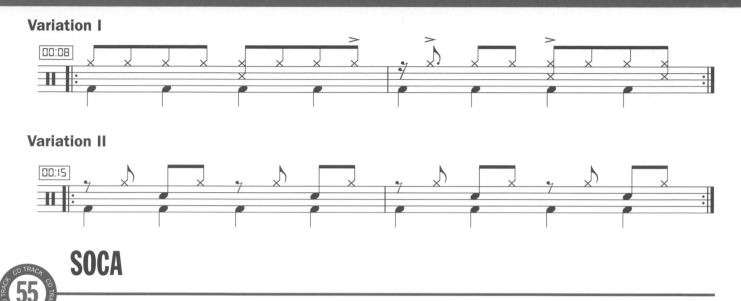

Variation II

SOCA

Soca is a rhythm from the island of Trinidad that became popular in the 1970s. It is essentially a faster, modern version of calypso.

Standard

Variation I

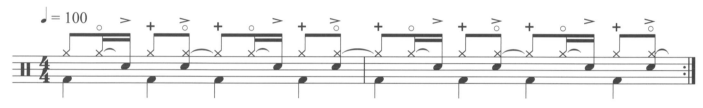

WALTZ

This Austrian dance in ¾ is still very popular today. The *waltz* rhythm started in the late eighteenth century, and reached its height of popularity in the middle decades of the nineteenth century.

Standard

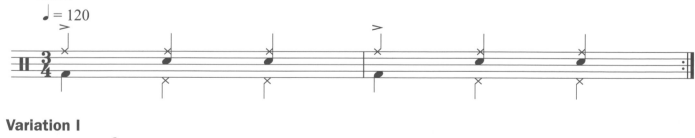

Variation I

WALTZ (continued)

56

Variation II

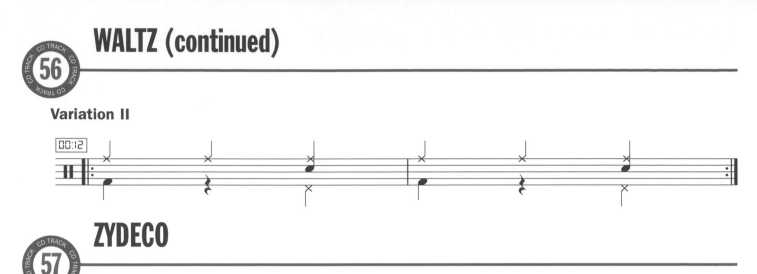

ZYDECO

57

Zydeco is a form of Louisiana Creole dance music closely related to Cajun, with Caribbean and African influences. Zydeco is played with a button accordion (or the less-traditional keyboard accordion) and a *frottoir* (a washboard or "rubboard" percussion instrument worn on the chest).

Two-Step

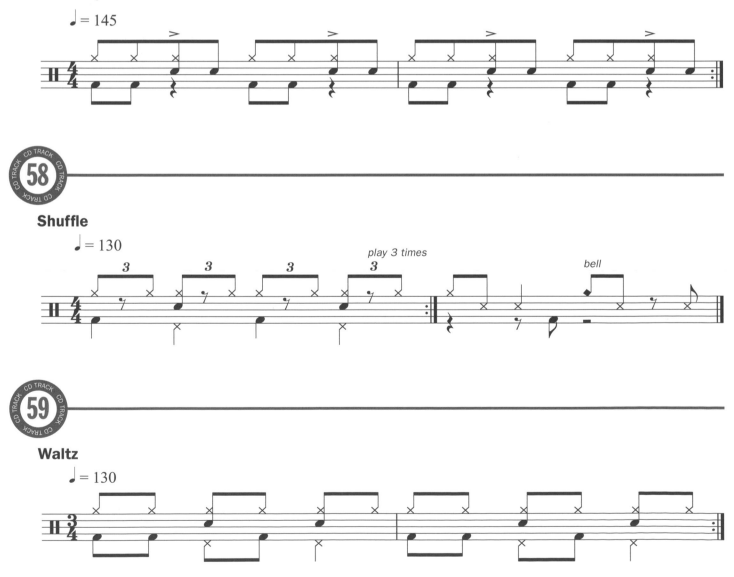

58

Shuffle

59

Waltz

TUNING AND MAINTAINING YOUR DRUMSET

Tuning

Tuning is the process of producing or preparing to produce a certain pitch in relation to another pitch. Since most percussion instruments are non-pitched, tuning refers to the relative highness or lowness of each instrument and serves to accentuate or diminish certain overtones according to taste.

In order to achieve the correct tuning of a certain group of drums, we must adjust one drum at a time by adjusting the tension on each drum head through the tightening or loosening of the *tuning lugs.*

After tuning one drum (adjusting for overtones and highness or lowness), we can then proceed to correctly tune the rest of the drums in relation to the first. This way, we are using the first drum as our *reference pitch.* The reference pitch for the first drum is typically obtained from a tuning fork, an electronic tuning device, a piano, or an oboe if you are playing in an orchestra.

The Snare Drum
Step 1: Cleaning the Snare Drum

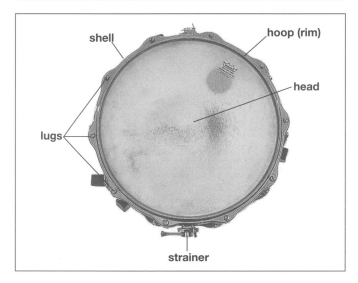

Use a clean, dry cloth to wipe off the hoop (rim) and the shell. Make sure you remove stick shavings, dust, and any buildup that may have accumulated in or around the edges. Clean the inside of the drum as well.

Place the head onto the shell and spin it around the edge to make sure there is nothing in between. Tighten the tension rods until they make contact with the hoop. Do not apply any pressure yet.

Make sure the snares are turned off. (The snares are a set of curled metal wires located on top of the bottom head.) The snare drum cannot be tuned with interference from the snares.

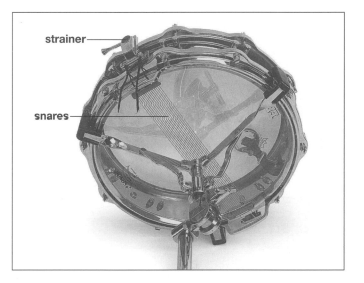

Step 2: Tuning

Always tune the top head first. Place the new head on top of the metal shell and turn each lug clockwise to increase the tension on the head, which raises the pitch of the drum.

The lugs have to be adjusted one at a time, always tuning the next lug located opposite of the first (180° away). By tuning the snare drum in this manner, we achieve uniform tension on all sides of the drum head. This tuning process is known as *opposite-lug sequence.*

TUNING AND MAINTAINING YOUR DRUMSET

The following diagrams show the tightening order for drums with four, six, eight, ten and twelve lugs. Follow these steps in order to achieve an even tension and accurate tuning.

Step 3: Fine-Tuning the Drum Head

Repeat the above tuning process on the bottom head. As you tighten the head, apply smaller increments of pressure (half and quarter turns) to the lugs. Because bottom snare drum heads are thinner and tend to break more easily, be careful not to tune it too high. Tap around the circumference of the head, listening for low-tuned areas. Test the pitch of each lug by lightly tapping about one inch away from the lug with a drumstick (some drummers prefer to use their fingertips). Listen carefully for the high and low spots. Tighten the low areas in order to achieve consistency. Try detuning each lug and then slowly tune it up again to try to match the pitches.

Snare Drum Tuning Tips

When tuning the snare drum, remember that the tighter the bottom head, the more the snares will vibrate, producing a drier sound. The looser the bottom head, the less the snares will vibrate. As a result, the drum will produce a loose, "fluffy" sound.

The vibration of the snares against the bottom drum head can also be adjusted by the tightness of the strainer, which is usually located on the side of the snare's shell. The tighter the strainer, the shorter the duration of the buzz; the looser the strainer, the longer the duration of the buzz.

Tune the bottom head to get a snare sound that will best accommodate your individual style of music. Some styles require a tighter sound, while others sound best with a loose buzz.

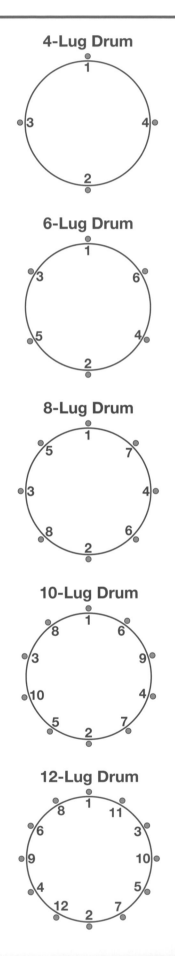

TUNING AND MAINTAINING YOUR DRUMSET

The Bass Drum

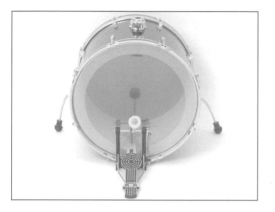

Step 1: Tuning the Front Head

The front head should always be tuned first. Since the tightness of this head doesn't greatly affect the overall sound of the bass drum, some drummers choose to tighten it just enough so it doesn't look wrinkled.

Step 2: Tuning the Back Head

Follow **Step 2** of the snare drum (opposite-lug) tuning sequence. The bass drum should not be tuned so high that it loses its characteristic deep, booming sound. Remember that before the electric bass was invented, the bass drum was used as the foundation of the low frequencies in the rhythm section. The bass drum sound should be appropriate for the style of music you are playing.

Bass Drum Tuning Tips

Test the pitch of the bass drum head with the bass drum pedal only. Smaller beaters or drum sticks can leave undesired marks that can alter the overall bass drum head performance. When tuning the bass drum, make sure that only the felt beater is hitting the head. Any other part of the pedal can easily break the head.

A small hole cut in the front head will let air escape after the head is struck. By doing this, the foot pedal is allowed to bounce at just the right amount. Otherwise, the pedal can bounce too much, resulting in unwanted double notes.

Adjust the internal damping by adding muffling material to the inside of the shell (see **Muffling** below). In addition to regulating air pressure, a small hole in your bass drum's front head will allow you to add or modify the amount of muffling material without having to open the bass drum each time.

The Toms

Step 1: Tuning the Bottom Head

Tune the bottom head of each tom first, following **Step 2** of the snare drum (opposite lug) tuning sequence.

Step 2: Tuning the Top Head

After tuning the bottom head, proceed to the top head. At this point, it is very important that you tune the toms in relation to the snare drum. Check the pitch of each tom so that the sound is consistent throughout. Follow **Step 3: Fine-Tuning the Drum Head** of the snare drum tuning section.

GENERAL GUIDELINES FOR DRUMSET TUNING

Pitch

There are three main ways of tuning any two-headed drum (with the exception of the bass drum):

1. Top and bottom heads at same pitch

This tuning gets the sound preferred by most drummers—a warm, invariable sound with lots of sustain and overtones.

2. Top head tuned at higher pitch

This tuning produces a deep sound with a constant pitch and few overtones.

3. Bottom head tuned at higher pitch

This tuning produces a rich and piercing sound that is full of sustain and not too many overtones.

NOTE: The two heads should be tuned only slightly apart. If the heads are tuned too far apart, the sound waves produced by both heads will cancel each other out, resulting in a "dead" snare or tom sound.

Muffling

Muffling can be used to eliminate unwanted overtones and to further customize the sound of your drums.

The most common (and cheapest) method for getting rid of extra overtones is to tape a small piece of tissue to the edge of the drum head. You can also cut rings from old heads and tape them on top of the new heads. Alternate damping material, such as foam rings, cotton, napkins, felt, etc., to achieve different sounds. If you use many mufflers, tape the desired material to the inside of the head so it does not obstruct your playing surface.

If your intention is to get a deeper, "dead" drum sound, apply more material on top of the heads (some drummers even cover the whole drumset). Any type of fabric works well for this particular purpose. The amount of material you use depends on how muted you want your drums to sound.

Many drummers use Mylar rings to beef up their sound. Another good option is to use Evans' Hydraulic Oil heads on the toms. For the bass drum, try stuffing a pillow, blanket, or some other sort of thick fabric inside the shell.

Other materials used to muffle drumsets include napkins, clothing, wallets, adhesive bandages, rubber, sheets, duct tape, tissues, yarn, paper, and money, to name but a few.

DRUMSET MAINTENANCE

Plastic and Acrylic Parts

Drum shells are generally made of wood, and are usually coated with some sort of plastic or lacquered finish. The best thing to clean these types of surfaces is mild hand soap and warm water. Glass cleaners and other ammonia-based products will leave the surface dry and dull.

Never use anything abrasive, such as scouring pads or steel wool. They will ruin the plastic finish and scratch the surface.

To add shine to the shells, use furniture polish or guitar polish. Drum manufacturers also make special polishing products.

Always transport your gear in proper cases to protect them from damage. Hardshell cases are the best, since they offer the most protection and will keep your equipment in mint condition the longest.

Metal Parts and Shells

Most, if not all of the hardware in your kit will be chrome plated (or some other variety of metal alloy—see your owner's manual). This chrome coating can easily be ruined. The best way to prevent rusting is to keep your drums dry and dust-free at all times (so avoid storing them in the basement).

After every use, make sure there is not any kind of moisture left on the metal surfaces (such as sweat, condensation, etc.).
Always use a soft, dry cloth to prevent scratches.

Wipe down your equipment at least once a week. This will help prevent the formation of rust and the buildup of dust particles. If you see rust, use a commercial rust remover immediately. The longer you wait, the more damage the rust will do to the surface. For severely rusted equipment, some recommend the use of tougher solvents like gasoline or Naptha. You can also try using commercial metal polish for any metal part (other than cymbals). For the special care of cymbals, see **Cymbals** below.

DRUMSET MAINTENANCE

Lugs

Dryness and rusting makes lugs stiff and difficult to move. If your lugs have seized, apply small amounts of petroleum jelly (or commercial sewing machine lubricant) into the lugs to free them. Apply the lubricant with a cotton swab or a toothpick and gently screw the tension rod in and take out the lug. Never use a silicone-based lubricant such as WD-40, as it will remove the old lubricant and dry up the lug faster.

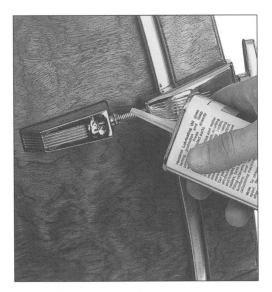

Cymbals

This is probably the most difficult and delicate part of the cleaning process. Cleaning and polishing your cymbals is all a matter of personal preference. Some drummers like to clean their cymbals regularly to keep them sounding bright and new. Others choose not to clean their cymbals, since they prefer a darker sound, and argue that cleaning the cymbal damages it since the polish removes metal. In reality, the amount of metal removed is minimal and not significant enough to damage the overall sound of the cymbal.

Use the brand of polish recommended by the manufacturer when cleaning your cymbals, as the materials, coatings, and finishes vary from one manufacturer to another. The recommended polish for one type of cymbal may damage or even ruin another, so always consult your owner's manual.

First, wipe off any loose dirt or dust with a commercial window cleaner. Use two clean cloths—one to apply the product and one to remove it.

Next, apply the correct polish carefully; most cymbal cleaners will remove the cymbal's logo if you wipe over them. Follow your cleaner's directions carefully, and apply small portions in a circular motion.

Clean off any excess polish with a commercial window cleaner, and buff with a soft, dry cloth.

Additional Tips

Car wax can be used to get rid of fingerprints. Apply small amounts of wax in a circular motion (following the cymbal's grooves), letting it dry to form a thin layer or haze. Buff with a dry cloth.

Always clean your cymbals after playing and before storing them. Carry your cymbals in a special hardshell case or cymbal bag. Do not let the cymbals touch each other during travel because friction between the surfaces could damage them.

123456